Michael Cardew

Michael Cardew

a collection of essays
with an introduction by Bernard Leach
and contributions by
Michael Cardew, Ray Finch,
John Houston and
Katharine Pleydell Bouverie

Distributed in the United States of America
and Canada by Watson-Guptill, New York

Crafts Advisory Committee

©1976 by Crafts Advisory Committee,
12 Waterloo Place, London SW1Y 4AU
The article by Katharine Pleydell
Bouverie is reprinted by permission
of *Ceramic Review*.

ISBN 0 903798 03 4 (paperback)
     0 903798 07 7 (hardback)

The pots were photographed by
David Cripps
Photograph of Michael Cardew
(frontispiece) by John Mahoney

Printed in Great Britain by
Lund Humphries

Contents

Acknowledgements

This book grew out of the preparations made for the first retrospective exhibition of Michael Cardew's pottery, held in 1976. The Crafts Advisory Committee is grateful to the many individuals and institutions whose assistance has made the exhibition, and this book possible: Edward Bawden; Katharine Pleydell Bouverie; Mariel Cardew; Michael Cardew; Alexander Cardew; Garth Clark; David Cripps; Ray Finch; Alister Hallum; Henry Hammond; Gwyn Hanssen; Dorothy Hope Smith; John Houston; W. A. Ismay; Dorris Kuyken-Schneider; Bernard and Janet Leach; Eileen Lewenstein; Philip Trevelyan; Muriel Rose; Cleo Witt; Moira Vincentelli. Thanks are due also to the directors of Bristol City Art Gallery and Museum; British Council; Cheltenham Art Gallery; Crafts Study Centre, Bath; Museum of English Rural Life, Reading; Stoke-on-Trent City Museum and Art Gallery; University College of Wales, Aberystwyth; Victoria and Albert Museum, London; York City Art Gallery and Museum.

Introduction

Bernard Leach is the most influential potter in this century. His work forms a bridge between European and Oriental traditions

When Hamada and I first started the Pottery at St Ives we had no idea of taking students.

Michael Cardew arrived after I'd gone home one evening in 1923. He accosted George Dunn who in turn informed Hamada. He must have been impressed, for he walked with Michael to my home in Carbis Bay a mile and a half away. I sounded him and he asked that very evening if he could come and work with us.

Handsome as a young Apollo with a straight Greek forehead and nose, curly golden hair and flashing blue eyes, Michael had a sudden temper, which disappeared nearly as fast as it arose! I shall never forget the first firing of the big climbing kiln, the third chamber of which contained some of his pots in English slip-ware; whilst unpacking the first and second chambers he could not disguise his impatience, so I let him take his own pots out of the third chamber. What he expected I've no idea, but there was no uncertainty of his dislike in what he saw. One after another his pots flew from his arm in a backward arc into the Stennack stream behind. Late that afternoon he was seen wading in the water retrieving what he could!

He had an exciting temperament between the two polarities of intellect and intuition; when the two came together the result was wonderful. Yet he was a lovable man. He was my first and best student.

From the very first his pots expressed the man. He, together with Hamada and I, rescued English slip-ware from entire loss. Michael spent thirteen years at Winchcombe making slip-ware before being appointed Chief Pottery Officer for Nigeria, where he took to high temperature stoneware for himself on the one hand, and defended the women potters in the country from exploitation on the other. Recently he did a film called *Mud and Water Man* for the Arts Council, in which may be seen the warmth of communication between 'man black' and 'man white'. I was so moved I reached for the phone and said, 'Michael, if you had never done anything else in your life, this film would have made it worth while.' My faith in him has never been shaken to its tap-root.

The Rose Bowl (shown opposite) he exhibited in Bond Street – now in Hanley Museum – I was allowed to place between two medieval English pitchers and say to the assembled students that it was not put to shame by them.

Bernard Leach
St Ives, Cornwall 1976

Bowl. Slip glazed earthenware, brown, cream and grey. Marks: MC and Winchcombe. D 37cm 1938. Hanley Museum, Stoke-on-Trent.

Winchcombe Pottery drawn by Thomas
Hennell to illustrate 'The Potter' in *The
Architectural Review*, 94, pp 49–51, 1943

The Early Years

John Houston, art critic and broadcaster, selected and documented
Michael Cardew's first retrospective exhibition

Michael Cardew's fifty-year-long career has acquired a legendary quality. His
work at Winchcombe between the two Wars now seems as remote and exotic as
the African experiences which followed, and filled his life for over twenty years.
He wryly acknowledges the legend, and suggests that it grew from his own absence
in Africa and the persuasive affection of Bernard Leach, whose wartime travels in
England incidentally conveyed an heroic image of Cardew's work. When Cardew
did return from the Gold Coast, ill and exhausted, in 1948, he found he was
famous, at least in the world of English pottery. The work he brought back and
exhibited the same year in his brother's London house, confirmed that fame. But
his plans to stay in England, to develop the Cornish pottery that he had built and
left ten years before, melted away when the chance came to return to Africa in
1950. This time he kept the route to England open, working at Wenford Bridge
each year on leave from Nigeria, and exhibiting his own and his Abujan pupils'
work in London. These migratory visits added substance to the legend, for only a
few people could conceive the whole sweep of Cardew's career, and there were
even fewer collections where his English earthenware could be seen beside the
African stoneware. His work at Winchcombe was naturally emphasised in the two
best informed reviews of modern pottery published in the 1950s: George
Wingfield Digby's *The works of the modern potter in England* (1952) and the
essential *Artist potters in England* (1955) by Muriel Rose.

The Potter's Book (1940) by Bernard Leach, in continuing post-war reprints,
included references to Cardew's work at Winchcombe. The coloured illustration
of the fountain bowl made in 1938 has fixed an image of Cardew as the natural
heir to the rich tradition of English slip-glazed earthenware. This image was
reinforced by the age and character of the Winchcombe Pottery, already a
century old when its production of flowerpots and milkpans stopped in 1915.
Cardew re-opened Winchcombe in 1926 and with two assistants made slipware on
the scale, and using the methods of a traditional country pottery. In 1942, with
Cardew about to leave for the Gold Coast, the pottery still represented the spirit
and the substance of an unbroken tradition, and was recorded as such by

Edwin Beer Fishley at the Fremington
Pottery, c.1907.

Thomas Hennell in an article for the *Architectural Review*. This was reprinted in
The Countryman at Work in 1947, and Hennell's words and drawings define a
selectively pastoral world in which the potter at Winchcombe takes his place
beside the rope maker, the hedger, the cooper and the thatcher. These country
craftsmen had retained their pre-industrial forms and methods in all essentials.
Their skills represented unbroken lines of succession. But in Cardew's case the
work developed from affinities that overpowered his education and social
environment. In choosing to become a potter, the most familiar pottery of his
childhood became a kind of raw material; although he was attracted by its
traditions, he did not seek to continue them. However, something of the
traditions re-emerged in Cardew's early work at Winchcombe, and the
circumstances that formed those traditions also reflect the increase of interest in
country pottery, and explain its presence in the prosperous Edwardian middle-
class home near Wimbledon Common, Cardew's home from his birth in 1901.

The Cardew family's country pots came from the Fremington Pottery in North
Devon, near enough to their holiday house at Saunton for visits to be made each
summer. Fremington was a family business, begun at the end of the eighteenth
century, and in the hands of Edwin Beer Fishley, the founder's grandson, from
about 1858 to his death in 1911. Bernard Leach calls Fishley 'the last English
peasant potter', and Hennell, drawing his words from Cardew, says 'He was
almost alone in maintaining the generous fancy of the old English potters and a
sense of style, through the most difficult period of transition and innovation.' This
difficult period affected Fremington, and many other country potteries in various
ways.

Fremington's staple, throughout its existence, was functional ware, mostly
vessels for the storage and preservation of food, such as six different sizes of
pitcher, large 'steins', pans for pickling meat and fish, and for scalding cream, and
jars for bread and 'barm' (the fermenting froth from malt liquor, used for
leavening bread). Ovens and baking dishes completed the range. The wares went
by wagon into North Devon or direct to Barnstaple market, and by sea, from the

Jug. Slip glazed earthenware, brown, incised in Cornish: TY POT A BRY, MUR MY A'TH-GAR NYNJES EN OL AN BYS DHE BAR: ('Thou noble pot, I love thee well. In all the world thee has no equal.') Marks: MC and St Ives. H 21cm *c.*1924–6. Edward Bawden.

Bottle with handle. Salt glazed stoneware,
brown. Marks: MC and St Ives.
H 18·5cm *c.*1924–6. University College of
Wales, Aberystwyth.

Fishley Quay, into the ports of Somerset and North Cornwall. The wares were cheap (in 1900 a fifteen-inch pan cost 3½d and an eight-pint pitcher, 7d) and largely undecorated. The baking dishes were combed to show the red clay beneath the white slip, but few other pots had more than a bead of moulding. Such wares were made to be broken and replaced.

The Gothic Revival had sponsored an interest in the English medieval, and later, applied arts. Pottery was among the last of the arts to be considered, but in the last quarter of the nineteenth century a number of books were published that showed the connections between the medieval tradition and surviving country potteries. The Fremington Pottery was mentioned in Llewellyn Jewitt's *Ceramic Art of Great Britain* (1878). This revival of interest focused on the more decorative traditional wares of the seventeenth and eighteenth centuries and slowly created a new market for the most versatile potters, like Fishley, who made brightly glazed puzzle jugs, tygs, porringers, and harvest jugs, all lavishly decorated with slip-trailed spots and spirals, and incised with rhymes and mottoes. These new 'old' wares were not only derived from English models. The journalist Hugh Strong, visiting Fremington in the late 1880s, noticed versions of Greek vases and 'clever imitations of Japanese and Egyptian designs, . . . the nucleus of a most profitable art industry'. Fishley's grandson, William Fishley Holland, worked at Fremington from 1900 to 1912. His autobiography *Fifty years a potter* (1958) describes the social changes which affected the pottery's production. An increasing number of homes had piped water, and this reduced the need for pitchers. Cheap galvanised and enamelled wares reduced the market even more. Cast-iron stoves and cooking equipment produced wide-reaching changes in the preparation of food: pottery ovens became redundant. Fremington maintained a steady trade, but had been unable to raise the price of its wares for many years. These were the pressures behind Fishley's search for new markets, but his delight in experimenting carried him beyond the production of nostalgic novelties. His new wares were glazed with red lead and oxides of copper and cobalt, and fired without saggars, so that the flames licked round the unprotected pots and added curious blooms and lustres to their surfaces. At the end of his life he spent all his time on this work. His grandson, in charge of the standard ware side of the pottery, speaks of strange experiments involving milk and treacle.

The Cardew family brought away both types of ware from their visits to Fremington. Pitchers and baking dishes for the kitchens at Saunton and Wimbledon, the gaudier wares to decorate the rest of the house. Michael scarcely remembers the visits (Fishley died in 1911, and his grandson left the pottery in 1912), but the pots remained as a powerful influence. In 1919 he went up to Exeter College, Oxford, to read Classics. His interest in pottery increased, and in 1921 he visited William Fishley Holland at the pottery he was managing at Braunton in North Devon. Cardew learnt to throw at Braunton, and spent an increasing amount of time there, working on his own when the pottery was closed. It was at Braunton, in the summer of 1922, that he first read about the new pottery at St Ives. The decision not to follow the professional career which his family expected must have been forming at this time, for when he visited St Ives, early in 1923, he asked Bernard Leach to let him join the pottery.

Bernard Leach (b. 1887) had returned to England from Japan in 1920. He had been born in China, and lived in Japan as a child, but came to England at the age of ten. Six years later he was the youngest student at the Slade School of Art, and in 1908 he was studying etching under Frank Brangwyn. He returned to Japan in 1909, intending to teach etching, and to study Eastern art. But in 1911 he took part 'at a sort of garden-party at an artist friend's house in Tokyo' in decorating some unglazed pots. These were glazed and fired in a little portable kiln, and within an hour from painting them Leach was handling his first raku pots. He describes the consequences in *A Potter's Book*: 'a dormant impulse must have awakened, for I began at once to search for a teacher and shortly afterwards found one in Ogata Kenzan, old, kindly and poor, pushed to one side by the new commercialism . . . and then living in a little house in the northern slums of Tokyo.' Leach's teacher was the sixth in a line of master-potters which had begun in the seventeenth century. From Kenzan, and from the many country potters he

Dish. Slip glazed earthenware, reddish brown. Marks: MC and Winchcombe. W 33cm c.1928. Katharine Pleydell Bouverie.

worked with while travelling about Japan, Leach absorbed a sympathetic and subtle knowledge for the materials and methods of his chosen craft. An extended stay in Peking and a visit to Korea widened his knowledge of Eastern methods. On his return to Japan in 1919 he met Shoji Hamada (b. 1892) who had just left the Institute of Pottery in Kyoto. When Leach returned to England to set up his own pottery, Hamada accompanied him.

The hospitality of the local handicraft guild helped them to become established in St Ives, and they built a small Japanese-style climbing kiln. They gradually discovered suitable material for their work, though many of their sources and methods of preparation were very different from those employed by the nearest 'English' potteries. In Japan, Leach had borrowed freely from the illustrations in Lomax's *Quaint Old English Pottery* (1909) to make raku ware which had something of the breadth and verve of seventeenth-century slipware. Now he searched for his native tradition directly, finding it in medieval jugs and pitchers, and in some of the simple, functional wares from the potteries such as Lake's at Truro.

Michael Cardew's enthusiasm was wholly for slipware. That January he visited Lake's pottery on his way to St Ives, met Hamada at the pottery and walked with him across the fields to Carbis Bay, where Leach lived. Cardew joined the pottery in July 1923, after taking his degree at Oxford. He brought with him two Devon traditions, the technique of pulled handles, and the kick wheel made for him at Braunton. This wheel, reduced in size and slightly modified, became the prototype of the ubiquitous Leach wheel. Cardew was responsible for a substantial part of the pottery's production of slipware. When he arrived the stoneware kiln was still being rebuilt and enlarged by Tsurunoske Matsubayashi, an engineer and chemist, who was also a potter. Cardew seems to have learnt mainly by instinct and intuition, by making and watching. His stoneware is recognisably like Leach pots at this time, compact and single-minded. The slipware is thrown generously and has great charm: golden brown and yellow jugs with Cornish inscriptions cut through the slip. But when the charm flowed too strongly from Fremington or

Dish. Slip glazed earthenware, yellowish brown. Winchcombe mark only. W 37cm 1928. University College of Wales, Aberystwyth.

Braunton, the result could be fussily quaint. Leach had visited the Cardew house at Saunton to inspect the Fishley pots, but he had turned away from the 'best' bright decorative wares and preferred the dishes in the kitchen.

Matsubayashi was the acknowledged authority on technical matters. In January 1924 Katharine Pleydell Bouverie (b. 1895) joined Cardew as a pupil at St Ives. In *Bernard Leach: Essays in Appreciation* (1960) she recalls 'At intervals Matsu had us all round the table taking notes while he lectured about kiln construction, chemical formulae or the plasticity of clay. "Velly important the cray should have the plasty" intoned Matsu, who never learned the difference between the letters L and R, but shook them up in a bag and took what came. "For which put in tub with water till smell bad, yes leally strike your nose too much, when have the plasty and perfect condition for make the cray body."' Cardew remembers the lectures with regret. He made few notes at this time; he thought theory did not matter. In June 1926 Cardew left St Ives and rented the

Three pages from Cardew's first kiln book at Winchcombe, 1927. 'Saggars' are fireclay trays and cylinders used to protect the pots from direct contact with the flames of the kiln. The diagram shows a kiln 'setting': the way in which the 'bungs' or columns of saggars were arranged in the kiln.

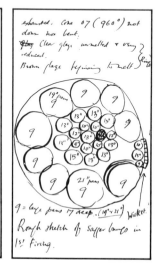

20

pottery at Greet, near Winchcombe, in Gloucestershire. It was about a century old, the same age as Fremington, but its range of earthenware had not extended beyond flowerpots and partly glazed pans when it closed in 1915. Cardew renamed it the Winchcombe Pottery. The first part of his article on page 55 describes what happened during his thirteen-year residence. On page 25, Ray Finch, who joined Winchcombe as a student in 1936, and has been its proprietor since 1945, recalls the excitement of firing the kiln in his early days there.

Cardew, like Leach, had to begin by finding suitable materials. After some difficulties he settled for the Fremington clay which Edwin Beer Fishley had used. This, with a very few slips and the traditional galena glaze, was all he needed throughout his years at Winchcombe. The first kiln book has survived. It records details of setting (putting the wares into protective saggars, and stacking these cylinders in tall pillars inside the kiln), and of firing (feeding the kiln with coal, then logs of wood, and finally fierce-burning faggots of larch and spruce, to raise

Mug and double dish with handle. Slip glazed earthenware, brown and cream. Mug: MC mark only; dish: MC and Winchcombe. Mug: H 9·5cm; dish: L 14cm. Mug: c.1929; dish: c.1930. Mug: Ray Finch; dish: Cheltenham Art Gallery.

the temperature inside the kiln to about 960°C after forty-eight hours of continuous work). There were eight firings in 1927, with successive kilns being better filled and better fired, and increasing from £25 4s 3d for 806 pots in the January kiln, to £66 13s 9d for 2248 pots in the eighth firing. Most of the items in each firing were the cheap flowerpots and milk pans that Comfort still produced. However, Cardew's own domestic pots, although representing only ten to fifteen per cent of the items in each kiln accounted for over sixty per cent of the value.

The kiln book also contains quickly-made pencil drawings of old pots and details of their decoration. The majority are Minoan, late and early, all full-bellied and narrow-footed, some with geometric decoration, but most with rippling patterns based on vines, flowers and marine forms. There is a similar, though coarsened character in the drawings of medieval pitchers from Oxford, Cheam and Aberystwyth. Cardew's own work absorbs these forms and broadens the rhythm of their decoration. Each pot adopts a single, simple theme, such as a broad undulating stripe of yellow wiped out of a darker slip to surround a substantial jug. When compared with his pots at St Ives these vessels have acquired a remarkable vitality, produced by the speed and certainty with which they were thrown. The work at Winchcombe develops from brisk pattern making, with slip trailed in symmetrical lines, dots and spirals, to the massive fountain bowls of 1938, on which the heavily glazed slip appears vaporous and scumbled. From the mid-nineteen-thirties his growing dissatisfaction with the limitations of slipware produced jars, bottles, and vases with harsher, taller forms. Sometimes heavy footed, they are the most massive pots made at that time. They are all dark in colour, most in rough black slip with deep slashes and freely incised patterns. Leach gives one of these pots a place in *A Potter's Portfolio* (1951) and describes it as 'built upon a right use of tradition which seems to me to have an equivalent life and value to Hamada's work in Japan. The fully developed shape and expressive throwing, the muscular certitude, the well spaced swinging pattern engraved through the raw glaze, and the springing handle all contribute to a living unity not unworthy of the eighteenth and earlier centuries'.

Jar with spigot. Slip glazed earthenware, black. Marks: MC and Winchcombe. H 37cm c.1935. Hanley Museum, Stoke-on-Trent.

Working at Winchcombe in 1936

Ray Finch, a student of Cardew's, owns and has run Winchcombe Pottery since 1945

Michael had already been working at Winchcombe for ten years when I came to the pottery as a student in January 1936. I had first seen some of his pots at the house of a friend, a year before, and this encounter was to change my whole life.

At that time the pottery workshop, dating from the early 1800s, consisted of one long low two-storey building, which also housed the big updraught bottle kiln. This dominated one end, the round chimney rising through the roof to six feet above the ridge and the chamber filling one quarter of the inside. On the ground floor, at the opposite end from the kiln, was a small workshop with two kick wheels where Elijah Comfort and Sidney Tustin worked. Between 'the Comfortry' as it was always called, and the kiln was Michael's workshop. Here stood, by the front window, a long knee-high wedging bench, a kick wheel, and in the corner opposite against the back wall, a power wheel driven by a petrol engine. The loft upstairs had a slatted floor so built to dry the pans and flowerpots made in earlier days. Here were now stored, in a variety of sizes, saggars from 15 to 53 centimetres in diameter, pans of glaze (on one piece of solid floor above the Comfortry), a kick wheel used by Charlie Tustin and racks of pots awaiting firing. Behind the pottery to the north was an open tiled shed for drying faggots and cordwood for the kiln, a horse-drawn pugmill and two small stone buildings for storing clay.

Michael had first used clay from the local brickyard with disastrous results; it was full of small pieces of limestone which 'blew' after firing. Clay was now dug from the orchard behind the pottery, as it had been for a hundred years or more, mixed with water pumped from the nearby brook into a slip and run over catchpits and through sieves into two covered, brick-lined settling pits. This was an early summer job and enough clay was washed in about three weeks to last a year. Before washing started, the previous year's clay, now more or less stiff, was dug from the pit and wheeled in barrows to the pugmill. It was a long day's work for everyone including the horse Nigger, who, harnessed to a long pole, and already familiar with cider mills, reluctantly trod a circular path and turned the pug. After pugging, the clay was stacked in the clay houses to sour.

Winchcombe Pottery c.1934. Left to right: Elijah Comfort, Charlie Tustin, Michael Cardew, 'Nigger' the horse who powered the pug mill and Sidney Tustin.

Sometimes Sidney and myself would spend a few days in the woods above Winchcombe binding up the trimmings from larch trees into bundles of 'faggots' as they were called. This was a pleasant job to which we both looked forward and had the added attraction of a little poaching on the side! Faggots were burned in the later stages of firing, their long flame helping to carry the heat to the upper part of the chamber. Quantities of cordwood too had to be sawn to length and stacked to dry.

The kiln was fired five or six times a year and by this time a wide range of standard ware was being produced. Michael would issue to each member of the team a list of pots to be made and the 'throwing' would begin. Smaller pots were made in runs of a hundred and upwards and each thrower made a number of shapes according to his capabilities and experience. Sidney, in his ninth year at the pottery, made small jugs, porridge bowls, eggbakers, soup pots, eggcups, butter-coolers, jam pots and so on. Mr Comfort was then about seventy; he had spent a lifetime making washing-pans and flowerpots and now made casseroles, lidded breakfast dishes, platters, round dishes and oval baking dishes in several sizes up to 48cm. These were made round; afterwards a piece was sliced from the middle, the dish made oval and rejoined. He also made saggars when replacements were needed. Charlie, the current apprentice in 1936, made honey pots and beakers whilst I, the complete novice, was set to make pressed dishes.

Michael's style was firmly established and he was making a wide variety of splendid pots; half and one gallon jugs, beer mugs, tea and coffee sets, store jars, teapots including large 'garden' teapots, cider jars from one gallon upwards, bowls of all sizes, and large fruit plates. Many still come to mind; a very large black cider jar with Adam and Eve and the serpent drawn through the raw glaze, a series of large rosebowls, two or three braziers with pierced decoration, a six gallon teapot on an iron stand, and numbers of bowls, dishes and plates with sgraffito or trailed slip birds, fishes or abstract patterns.

All the pots were once-fired and it was necessary to glaze the raw clay at a certain stage of dryness; if too dry the pots cracked, if too damp the glaze later

Jug. Slip glazed earthenware, ochre.
Incised: WINCHCOMBE. Winchcombe
mark only. H 15cm *c*.1930. Cheltenham
Art Gallery.

'skipped' from the rims or edges of handles. So during the making period glazing went on as required. Four very simple clear lead glazes were in use; three were of similar composition, ground galena (the natural lead ore) plus clay and flint. The so-called 'standard glaze' contained both white ball clay and local red clay, the iron oxide in the latter giving an amber colour over a white underslip. The 'white galena glaze' was made up with ball clay only; the 'green glaze' was identical with the addition of 3 per cent of copper oxide. In the fourth glaze a lead frit was substituted for galena; this glaze was only used for reglazing pots to be refired.

To cover the red firing clay before glazing there were two slips, a white slip made from Dorset ball clay and a black slip made from the local clay darkened with iron and manganese oxides. They were used both as dipping slips and, in a thicker consistency, as trailing slips. The methods of decoration were either slip trailing, most often white slip on black, or sgraffito through white slip. Sometimes black slip was painted on a nearly dry white slip and occasionally white slip direct onto the unslipped clay. With varying thicknesses of slip, the three different coloured glazes, and the added transmutations of wood firing, these simple techniques gave considerable variety of possible effects.

The throwing, decorating, and glazing period would take around seven to eight weeks. The ware was then placed in saggars and the saggars set in the nine foot diameter chamber in 'bungs' six feet high. The setter would begin to the right of the wicket or chamber entrance with the largest saggars and work round the chamber wall to the wicket again. Successive inner incomplete circles followed until the central bung was in place; thereupon he completed each circle in a reverse order until the chamber was filled. Michael nearly always set the kiln himself while Sidney and I filled saggars outside and carried them to the kiln. Charlie's special job at this time was rolling 'snakes' or wads from fire clay, to go between each saggar and at regular intervals Michael would shout: 'MORE snakes Charlie'. The six-foot high bungs were closed with a flat lid and stood level with the chamber walls; this left a large area under the curve of the dome to be filled.

Three-handled jar. Slip glazed earthenware, green and cream. Marks: MC and Winchcombe. H 32cm 1931. University College of Wales, Aberystwyth.

This was done by a system known as 'topping off' and involved building further circles of quite small saggars, upside down over small bowls, with each circle chequered over the one below to act as a baffle to the flames.

When the chamber was full Mr Comfort would brick up the wicket and cover it with soft clay and sand clamming. A loose brick was left, the spyhole opening into a long tunnel reaching four feet into the chamber; at the end stood three Seger cones, the top one on bending would indicate 1020°C and glazed trial rings, which were drawn with a long iron rod at intervals towards the end of the firing.

The workshop was cleaned, the fires laid, and six barrow-loads of coal wheeled in to each fire mouth. Cordwood was also stacked near the kiln and all was made ready. The fires were lit very early in the morning. Mr Comfort would keep a slow fire all day rising to a moderate fire by evening. If there were large pots in the kiln this slow fire might be extended by twelve hours or more, the kiln being lit the evening before. At 5 pm Mr Comfort went home and Michael took over. A kiln log was made out, a friend of Michael's would arrive to help with the stoking, Mariel would appear with a basket of good food and we settled down to a long night. By 9 or 10 o'clock a few pieces of cordwood were added to the coal stokes and by midnight we peered through a spy hole in the chimney to look for faint 'colour' at the vents in the dome. When this was clearly seen, indicating a temperature of over 600°C in the chamber, we changed to all wood stokes.

At 6 am Sidney and Charlie arrived with two extra men hired for the day and, whilst the last of the cordwood was burnt, bundles of faggots were carried in. Now four stokers were needed, one to each fire mouth, each man equipped with wire cutters and a long wooden-handled, two-pronged fork. The binding wire on the faggot was cut and hung on a post to record the number burnt – sufficient taken to nearly fill the fire mouth, thrown onto the fire bars and pushed with the fork right into the firebox. The brushwood burst into flame and was quickly consumed sending a rush of flame right up through the chamber and, at the height of firing, out of the chimney. It was a very hot, dusty and exhausting job, spectacular indeed but not over efficient.

Vase. Slip glazed earthenware, green and
cream. Marks: MC and Winchcombe.
H 32cm 1931. University College of
Wales, Aberystwyth.

The stoking was continuous for about forty minutes when Michael would shout – 'Cool off'–. This however referred more to the kiln than to the stokers, for then the glowing embers at the firebacks were raked forward, the hot ashes dug from the ashpits, and more faggots carried in. For up to eight minutes the kiln was not stoked, this prevented over-firing the bottom and helped the heat to rise in the chamber.

Michael, wearing an old boiler suit and a black beret, directed operations. From time to time he climbed up and looked through the spy into the chimney where he could see the flames rising from each fire; 'More Number Two' he would shout or – 'Quieter Number Four'.

The stoke and cool off periods continued throughout the day until it was judged time to look in; the brick in the wicket was removed, the cones observed, and a trial ring drawn. The full fire went on until the last cone was bending and the glaze on the rings well melted. The fierce bursts of flame from faggot stoking often produced local or general reduction to which the lead glazes reacted at once by bubbling violently. Care was always taken to finish the kiln with gentle oxidising annealing stokes which helped any blisters to subside.

At last after perhaps forty hours or more the firing finished. The fire mouths were covered with iron plates and clammed up with clay. Finally a damper was lowered by chain and tackle onto the top of the chimney and the kiln left to cool. But the hazards were not yet over; someone had to sleep near the kiln, with a hosepipe to hand, in case fire should break out in the rafters near to the intensely hot chimney.

After three anxious days of waiting the clamming was broken, the wicket taken down and the kiln drawn. The risks of firing were still high and it is difficult to convey the excitement – and disappointments – of unpacking a kiln of this size, the climax of so many weeks of work.

They were indeed memorable days.

Teapot. Slip glazed earthenware, brown and cream. Marks: MC and Winchcombe. W (handle to spout) 40cm *c.*1933. Katharine Pleydell Bouverie.

A Personal Account

Katharine Pleydell Bouverie studied with Cardew at Bernard Leach's. In 1925 Matsubayashi helped build the kiln at her Coleshill pottery

Michael Cardew at the wheel at Winchcombe, c.1934.

Four-handled jar. Slip glazed earthenware speckled yellow and brown. Marks: MC and Winchcombe. H 30cm c.1935. Hanley Museum, Stoke-on-Trent.

The Cardews had a holiday house at Saunton in North Devon. Fremington lay a few miles away along the sands, and sometimes in fine weather the whole family would walk over and picnic there, and visit the pottery where E. B. Fishley was still working; and wander home through the golden evenings of before the First World War, laden with yet more Fishley pots. Michael can barely remember these picnics, and he was only ten when Fishley died. But Fremington pots were still treasured in the Cardew house; and although he did not realize it at the time, he was already securely hooked.

Because he was clever and classical minded it seemed natural that some sort of academic life lay ahead of him. So when he left school he went up to Oxford with a scholarship. But he got into trouble with the authorities because, instead of attending to his books as a good scholar should, he spent his vacations at Braunton, learning to throw under Fishley's grandson Holland, and working in the pottery on the understanding that he could practise on the wheels when the place was shut. It happened, therefore, that the degree in Greats that should have been a first was a third. And when all that was over Michael bicycled down to St Ives where Bernard Leach was struggling with a mountain of difficulties up the Stennack Hill, met Leach and Hamada, and enrolled as Bernard Leach's first English apprentice. That was towards the end of 1923.

It was at St Ives, a few weeks later, when Hamada was packing up to return to Japan, that I first met Michael. I had been accepted, generously if rather reluctantly, as a second apprentice; and we spent 1924 together, working under Bernard's erratic but mainly genial tutelage. The team consisted of Bernard himself, his partner-secretary Edgar Skinner, a gentle and charming old man whose business training landed him in a perpetual flutter about the pottery's finances; Tsurunoske Matsubayashi, a young Japanese who had just started to rebuild the first stoneware kiln; Michael; George Dunn, a ribald nautical character who did a good deal of the heavy work and told horrific smuggler's tales in broad Cornish, and me. Peter Mason, another girl and my first partner at Coleshill, worked part time.

Michael at that time was twenty-two, loped about in a disjointed way and looked like one of the less Archaic Kouroi that stand round the walls in Greek museums. He was already a capable thrower and a prodigious worker: he would make up vast quantities of clay and then disappear into a little shed and turn them into the plates and bowls and curly-handled mugs and jugs which, until the stoneware kiln was finished, formed a large part of the pottery's production wares. At one stage during the year he contracted pneumonia, a habit that has pursued him through life; and returned to us with a good deal of the convalescent's irritability and all of a convalescent's hunger. There was a memorable moment when he burst into the main shed where Bernard was throwing on the Japanese stick wheel, snarled 'Isn't there going to be any lunch today?', and grabbed the handle of the cupboard where the utensils were kept. The handle stuck; the top half of the cupboard came adrift and swung forward. Then the doors opened and there was a small cascade of crockery. Michael, with a heave and a grunt of pure rage, pushed the cupboard back into position and stormed out of the shed. Whoever was in fault in this matter of lunch – probably me – got busy with some speed.

Michael was at St Ives for three years; and then, almost by chance, stumbled across the derelict pottery at Greet, near Winchcombe, and, on a capital of £300, rented it from the Butlers, who owned the farm.

He did some repairs to the kiln, enticed Elijah Comfort back from the plough and restored him to his wheel, and set about bringing the Winchcombe Pottery into being. He had every trouble proper to beginners: his first big load of clay was dumped, inexplicably, on to a pile of coal dust and the carbon 'blew' in the body. He tried the local brickclay, good enough for bricks but containing lime so that they blew too. The farmer would not let him dig clay in the farm orchard, a prohibition perhaps not surprising. And the worn-out kiln could not be fired high enough to eliminate severe porosity. But somehow he made some good pots. He lived in fantastic discomfort, first in the pottery loft and later in a wooden shack in the orchard where he was not allowed to dig. As far as I remember his

Jar. Slip glazed earthenware, black.
Marks: MC and Winchcombe. H 35·5cm
c.1936. Hanley Museum, Stoke-on-Trent.

bath was a huge cask of rainwater beside the only door. I am not sure what happened when there was no rain; but the Cotswolds have a wettish climate. He had some relaxation; like all his family he played various instruments – clarinet – recorder – rebeck and he folk-danced enthusiastically with the Gloucestershire team, even to the extent of dancing with them at the national festivals in the Albert Hall. And when Peter put *Everyman* on in a twelfth-century barn near our pottery (Winchcombe and Coleshill are not all that far apart), he came and played the Angel for us. He looked rather fine in Fra Angelico colours up in the loft; and he shared the loft with a hen who laid an egg and announced the fact while he welcomed Everyman into heaven.

But, mainly, he worked. He did not, I think, make much money; but he began to make a name. And as the years passed he made pots of an increasing magnificence, firing them harder as he got around to rebuilding the kiln. Gradually there were exhibitions, group shows at first and then shows on his own. By 1932 both the Tustin brothers were working for him as well as Elijah, so production increased.

In 1933 he married Mariel Russell, who was a marvellous person and looked like Pomona. She still is, and does. And in 1934 Seth was born, and baptised (in November) in a Cotswold stream. They continued to live in the hut till, with the advent of Cornelius and Ennis, they outgrew it and moved to a cottage nearby.

I suppose the Cornishman in Michael was always hungry for granite and the sea. Anyhow, in 1939 he bought the old inn at Wenford Bridge near Bodmin, and moved there just before the phoney war began. He built a smaller version of the Winchcombe kiln and started firing about the time when Holland and France fell; and during the next couple of years made slipware under the increasingly difficult conditions of the shooting war.

However, the boys grew and needed to be educated, so both parents went off to make some money, Mariel to teach in Buckinghamshire, Michael to take over Harry Davis's job at Achimota College in what is now Ghana. Mariel achieved her object of making some money: Michael did not, since the crafts side of

Oval dish. Slip glazed earthenware, yellow, green, brown and black. Winchcombe mark only. W 29·5cm c.1938. Bristol Art Gallery.

Achimota, conceived on too ambitious a scale, came to an end and Michael was out on his neck. He stayed on in Ghana, started a small pottery at Vumé, learned the hard way about Africa's raw materials, and more or less starved on £120 a year. ('Oh yes, eggs and coconuts and cassava and palm oil. Full of vitamins.')

The vitamins did not preserve him from median otitis, poisoned hands and some more pneumonia. Also during the 'troubles' in 1948, he only escaped murder at the hands of a gang from another province because his local chief warned him not to stay at home, so that it was merely his mosquito net that was stabbed in the night. He came back to England at the end of that year looking rather more than half dead.

He began then to make stoneware at Wenford, adding a downdraught first chamber to the kiln. In 1949 Ivan McMeekin turned up from Australia and joined him. But later in that year there was an advertisement for a Pottery Officer for Nigeria. Michael hesitated, applied, thought he had lost the chance, found he had not; and was off again in 1950, this time on the job that was to last for the next sixteen years. 'And I was fifty. And that was when my life began.'

Thereafter, from the point of view of his friends in England, he always seemed to be coming or going. He would arrive, each time a little more burnt out and emaciated, but perenially interested, enthusiastic and amused. He was at Bernard's Dartington conference in 1952, when the vagaries of his 'all ball' wheel reduced one famous American potter to the verge of hysteria. He brought home from Africa impressive exhibitions which were put on at the Berkeley Galleries, sometimes his own pots, sometimes those of his students too. He also brought the students, Kofi from Ghana, Ladi Kwali from Abuja, to demonstrate their admirable skills. He ran his own hilarious 'Geology for Potters' course at Wenford in 1959; when thirty or so of us roared round Cornwall in cars and jeeps and vans collecting peculiar raw materials from mines and quarries; and listened in the evenings, when not too stupified by air and sun, to his close-packed and concentrated lectures. Incidentally it was straight on top of that course that he

Teapot. Glazed stoneware, bronze and
rust. Marks: MC and Volta. H 17cm
1947–8. Alexander Cardew.

Jug, made as prototype for industrial
production, seal with 1951 applied.
Glazed stoneware, grey-green. Marks:
MC and Wenford Bridge. H 20·5cm
1950. Ray Finch.

was found to be infected with Bilharzia, so that he spent the next weeks enduring a rather grisly cure in the Hospital for Tropical Diseases in London. Ordered never again to bathe in the River Iku, he returned to Abuja and bathed in the Iku with complete impunity for the next six years.

All good things come to an end; and such eventualities as retiring age arrive for us all. So the job as Pottery Officer came to an end in 1965; and in June Michael was back in England again. Not, of course, for long. By the beginning of 1968 he was off to Australia, to help Ivan, now at the University of New South Wales, to start a pottery for the Aborigines in the Northern Territory. And he was away all that year.

Now, at seventy-four, he roves about the world, teaching, lecturing, running summer schools and geology courses; taking things as they come and enjoying them. Almost always enjoying. His complete absence of self-advertisement leads him, at times, into comic situations: it was while godfathering Kofi and Ladi round some of the American Universities that a kind lady, helpfully bringing him into the picture, asked: 'Then, Mr Cardew, do you make pottery too?'

I imagine that the goblin at his shoulder has always been Edward Lear. Natural enough, since it was his great-aunt who loved Lear and was loved by him, though they never got around to marrying. The influence shows in many ways; in his always individual attitude to things, his oblique sense of humour, his wanderings about the Great Gromboolian Plain. In some of his more personal pot decorations, too: the solemn fish; the slightly sinister owls indicated in two lines on goblets; the ostrich on a plate making a face at a wisp of thistledown. And at any moment he may quote Lear by the yard.

And, like Lear again, wherever he goes he makes friends: whenever he talks people laugh. He has written one of the best books on the making of pots in the English language. And he has made pots. His odd and erratic career is littered with them. Steeped in tradition, but tradition always freely used; pots made because the potter wanted to make them; made for use; idiosyncratic, sometimes funny, often splendid. No mean achievement, one would suppose.

Africa and Cornwall

John Houston

Cardew's London exhibition at the Brygos Gallery in 1938 was virtually his last public appearance in England for ten years. He found the situation at Winchcombe frustrating. The old kiln was incapable of reaching the temperatures that he felt his new work required. The living quarters had always been primitive – a barn loft entered by ladder and trapdoor, and a hut in the orchard – and the only cottage available had proved even worse for his growing family. The cultural life of the district still centred on Chipping Campden with its memories of C. R. Ashbee's Guild of Handicraft. Cardew had exhibited at the Cotswold Gallery in Soho Square. This London showcase for many of the Cotswold craftsmen was run by A. J. Finberg, the artist and Turner scholar, whose son Herbert had founded the Alcuin Press in Campden in 1928. But the energetic simplicity which had characterised the best work made in the Cotswolds before the first World War, now only survived among certain makers of furniture. The other crafts had dwindled to an obsession with the 'exquisitely wrought'. Cardew remembers that he was thought to be 'a complete Yahoo'. His affection for Cornwall, which extended beyond the time spent at St Ives, to his own family's origins, and his knowledge of the Cornish language and traditions, guided the search for a new home.

In 1939 he bought Wenford Bridge, previously a public house, which formed a group of traditional stone-walled buildings close to a stream of the River Camel in a deep valley on the fringe of Bodmin Moor. He built a smaller version of the Winchcombe kiln and experimented with tin-glazed earthenware for a short time. He had formed a partnership with Ray Finch, who was now running the Winchcombe pottery, and it was planned to preserve the links between the two businesses. But the commencement of war that year changed everything for Cardew. Wartime restrictions inhibited the growth of any non-essential business, and quickly threatened the continuance of Winchcombe too. Cardew returned there in 1941. In 1942 he was asked to suggest a potter for a scheme in West Africa. He accepted the job himself.

The Achimota College Pottery Unit is described by Cardew on page 60. Some

Cardew and Clement Kofi Athey in Cardew's bungalow at Abuja. Kofi had worked at the Volta Pottery and became Cardew's chief assistant at Abuja.

45

The Volta Pottery at Vumé-Dugamé in 1947. The main chamber of the stoneware kiln is inside the thatched building in the centre. In the foreground is part of the huge woodstack.

Dish. Glazed stoneware, grey-green. Marks: MC and Wenford Bridge. D 26cm 1949. British Council.

of the background to his enthusiasm for the ill-fated scheme and his admiration for H. V. Meyerowitz, its initiator, can be found in his own article 'Industry and the Studio Potter' in the magazine *Crafts* in 1942. At one stage of his dissatisfaction with Winchcombe he had wanted to work within the pottery industry. He had discussed the idea with William Staite Murray, then Head of the Pottery School at the Royal College of Art, but Murray, whose conception of pottery was as a form of abstract art, offered the discouraging maxim 'you cannot make love by proxy'. Industry was equally discouraging, though a kindly director at Copelands allowed him to work at the Stoke-on-Trent factory for six weeks in 1938, making tea sets in 'fine earthenware'. In his article Cardew argued that few designers for industry knew anything about pottery, and that the potteries were organised to manufacture designs by isolating and directing a neutral process referred to as 'pure craftsmanship'. Such organisation was based on a fallacy, there being no such thing as 'pure craftsmanship'. He suggested that any good small pottery was potentially a better factory, since the elements of standardisation and repetition were essentially involved as part of a single activity. His objections were not to the division of labour, but to the emasculating separation of thought from action. Meyerowitz's pottery scheme at Achimota was planned to respect this essential unity. He believed that the African craftsmen's own culture would eventually transform their new skills. But only if the skills were taught by men who could convey the potential richness of their craft.

Meyerowitz died in 1945 and the scheme was abandoned. Cardew's grief and disappointment were severe. He chose to remain in the Gold Coast and with the money he took instead of his passage home, he and three African students travelled to Vumé-Dugamé, about twenty miles inland on the Lower Volta River. The village had about one thousand inhabitants and had long been a centre of pottery production. These local pots were hand built with coils of clay and fired in open heaps. As in most of West Africa, the women were the potters. The kiln and the potter's wheel were unknown. Here Cardew and his helpers built the Volta

Liquid clays and glazes were stored in large local pots, sunk in the ground between the kiln shed (left) and the glaze mill (right), at Vumé.

Jar. Glazed stoneware, bronze and rust. Marks: MC and Volta. H 24·5cm 1947–8. British Council.

pottery, making their own bricks, prospecting for raw materials, building the kiln, testing glazes and clays. The preparation took two years.

The clay used for the local pots formed the basis of their own stoneware body. The glaze made use of the piles of oyster-shells which had accumulated at one end of the village and a natural iron oxide became the chief pigment. Most of Cardew's own pots made at Vumé are sleekly glazed in dark bronze-green. The iron decoration flares from deep rust to orange. The forms are restrained, the glaze is immaculate, the pots themselves are all modest in size. The contrast between these pots and the last work made at Winchcombe is very great, and the essential difference seems a matter of concentration. The finest of the few Vumé pots in England seem inimitable, whereas the exuberance of the best work at Winchcombe suggested a multiplicity of likenesses.

In 1948, after six years in the Gold Coast, Cardew became ill and was forced to return to England for treatment. The pots he had brought were exhibited at his brother Philip's London House. Cardew returned to Wenford Bridge and rebuilt his kiln, adding a downdraught first chamber in order to continue his work in stoneware. The work he made in 1949 revised some of the themes of his work at Volta, but with a more rugged body and in paler greys and blues. The flagons, pitchers and almost spherical jars, were basically Winchcombe forms. But compared with their earthenware prototypes they seemed thin skinned and underdone.

As work at Wenford got under way the possibility of work in Africa recurred. In 1950 he became Pottery Officer in the Nigerian Department of Commerce and Industry, and set out to survey the resources of the Northern region, an area comparable in size to the whole of the British Isles. He travelled several thousands of miles, observing and collecting the traditional pottery, and taking samples of clays and rocks. The Nigerian pots were all made by the same basic coiled techniques as those at Vumé-Dugamé. They were entirely suitable for their traditional uses, but these traditions were becoming overlaid with new ways of storing, cooking and eating food. The situation had elements in common with

Abuja in the 1960s. The kiln chimney is in the centre. The circular building on the right is of traditional local design.

those that had diminished the role of English country potteries, such as Fremington, some fifty years before. Earthenware had lost its place as a cheap and convenient material when increasing quantities of galvanised and enamelled metal objects became available. Although some studio-potters, notably Leach and Cardew, had chosen to work in earthenware, their example did not revive its popularity as a domestic material. Cheap metal also threatened the traditional pottery of Africa. In 1936 Meyerowitz had noted, in his *Report on the possibilities of development in Basutoland,* that traditional pottery skills were fading in 'paraffin tin-stricken areas'. At that time he had proposed the creation of a cultural centre for the Bantu. The centre was to be staffed, under the guidance of a European artist, by Bantu technical experts who could guide the students through the cultural complexities of their own arts and crafts, but without interfering with the artistic merits or demerits of the work produced. Meyerowitz particularly recommended a kiln for the centre.

Cardew's written survey on the prospects of pottery in Nigeria was well received by his Department. His Pottery Training Centre at Abuja was opened in April 1952. There were six African trainees. Abuja lies at the centre of Nigeria, and during the six-month rainy season the grass plain, rain clouds, and the sound of the river at the edge of the pottery site, reminded Cardew of the West of Ireland. The pottery grew and prospered. In 1962 there were thirteen potter's wheels and a group of potters who remained permanently at Abuja while the trainees moved on at the end of their four-year course.

Cardew spent nine or ten months each year in Nigeria, working at Abuja, visiting past trainees, establishing another pottery school at Jos, and helping to build part of the museum there. Many of his own pots, at first sight, seemed to have regained some Winchcombe characteristics. Brisk incisions were sketched through the glaze, creating rough, pale ridges that caught the light and sparkled like bright-cut engraving. Glazed storage jars, some of them 60 or 70 centimetres high, were patterned with intersecting curves and tall leaf forms. Inevitably, Cardew's pots absorbed his African experience: tea pots and casseroles acquired tall collars around their lids; a series of seats which derived from kingship stools were built from upturned vase shapes, each surrounded by a cage of a dozen or more long pulled handles. In general the Abujan work was dark in tone, grey-greens, blacks, and bronzes, and often with lively variations in the glazes.

He worked at Wenford Bridge for about two months each year, and though the lively sgraffito decoration was less evident, there was an increasing range of relationships between bodies and glazes. The forms of wide bowls and tall lidded pots became tauter and tougher, as though the stoneware body was under stress. Some glazes – at both Abuja and Wenford – were allowed to run thinly in even vertical stripes, creating varying opacities of grey and green which chequered the prominent throwing rings on narrow jars.

Teapot with screw lid. Glazed stoneware, reddish brown. Marks: MC and Abuja. W (handle to spout) 17·5cm *c.*1956. Ray Finch.

In 1965 he retired from Abuja, and settled, for the third time, at the Wenford Bridge Pottery. In the last ten years new themes have developed: broad bowls decorated with slanting stripes and dots of impasted glaze, like a basket pattern. Taller bowls, as massive as the 'fountain' wares made before the War, provide cool grey forms for strips of brush decoration in red and blue. In Africa, his tall storage jars seemed to recall the spontaneity and force of his best work at Winchcombe, ampler in form and more luxuriant in decoration, suggesting new rhythms.

The dominant quality of Cardew's work is its spontaneity. Bernard Leach refers to 'muscular certitude', and the phrase suggests the powerful co-ordination of instinct and experience which gives Cardew's pots their unrivalled energy of expression – an energy contained and controlled within the best pots, near to the edge of recklessness in others. But there are no sudden jolts of consciously sought influence or experiment. Instead, the pots have grown naturally from his different working situations. His work at Braunton, St Ives, and Winchcombe resulted from an affinity with a particular way of making pots. He did not search for a tradition, he was already absorbed by the need to work as a potter. He looked for situations where such work would be natural – and became a country potter.

In many ways he is a country potter still. After the grandiose failure of the Achimota scheme, with its hope of a reborn culture, and its expectation of 181,000 pots a year, his potteries at Volta and Abuja marked a return to the basic elements of his craft. English country potteries, such as Fremington and Braunton, had been the catalyst for his energies in the 1920s. Twenty-five years later his study of the materials in his West African environments provided the source, as well as the means of his work. His *Pioneer Pottery* (1969) is a by-product of that study, but the prime function of his researches was not to improve the efficiency of techniques but to respond more directly to the inherent qualities of his materials. His career began as a search for the means to work; it continues as an exploration of the nature of those means. His example and his influence is to turn potters back to their own materials as the prime source of work.

Plate. Glazed stoneware, brown and green. Marks: MC and Abuja. D 27cm c.1960. Katharine Pleydell Bouverie.

Slipware and Stoneware

Michael Cardew

Cardew unpacking the kiln at Wenford Bridge in 1972.

Soy pot with spout and screw lid. Glazed stoneware, brown. Marks: MC and Abuja. H 9·5cm c.1958. W. A. Ismay.

Oil jar with screw top. Glazed stoneware, green and white. Marks: MC and Abuja. H 23cm c.1959. W. A. Ismay.

The old pottery at Winchcombe which used to be called Greet Potteries or Beckett's Pottery, was closed early in the First World War, and had been lying idle for about twelve years when I first rented it in 1926. There was a big updraught kiln of the sort used in country potteries; the main chamber had a diameter of about 3 metres and a capacity between 14 and 17 cubic metres. During the Beckett era it was used for firing large earthenware washing-pans (which were glazed on the inside) and for flowerpots of all sizes. They also made bread-crocks, milk pans and cream pans.

During the thirteen years that I worked there I was making a kind of *slipware* – that is, a soft-fired galena-glazed earthenware. Galena is pulverised lead-ore (lead sulphide) and when properly fired combines with the free silica and clay of the pots, to give a nice yellowish glaze which is a warm chestnut brown over the natural red clay, yellow when applied over a white slip or a sort of black if used over a black slip. (Our black slip was the local red clay with added oxides of iron and manganese.) We did not use the galena by itself but mixed it with a small proportion of ground flint (about ten per cent) and plenty of clay, about thirty per cent, which enabled us to use it on the raw *black-hard* pots without having to give them a biscuit-fire beforehand. If red clay was used for this glaze it gave a bright yellow colour over the white slip. When we wanted a paler colour than the standard yellow we used white clay instead of red, and this gave a light cream colour. For green glaze we added five per cent of copper oxide to the 'cream' glaze.

There were only these three glazes, and they all had essentially the same composition; but owing to the method of firing there was a great range of fortuitous variations in colour: light or dark, or spotted and speckled with greens or yellows, or a golden brown like autumn leaves. Sometimes a patch of greenish colour was due, not to copper but to local areas of reduction-firing. Circular markings in a lighter red colour were often produced by minute particles of organic matter which were burnt out of the clay during the firing, giving rise to 'haloes' of local oxidation. We used to burn immense quantities of larch faggots during the final six or eight hours' stoking. The poking-in of these faggots, and the periodic raking-out of the mounds of incandescent embers which accumulated in the ashpits of each of the four 'fire-eyes' or stoke-holes, caused showers of uncontrolled sparks and fly-ash to rise up through the whole of the setting – it was these conditions which gave rise to the great variety in the colours.

It is sometimes stated that at Winchcombe I revived the English slipware tradition; but the credit for that belongs to Bernard Leach during the early years of the Leach Pottery at St Ives. What was special at Winchcombe was that we were making slipware on the scale of a real country pottery, in a kiln of the traditional size and design. But the kind of slipware which we made was rather different from the slip-trailed, 'combed' and 'feathered' pots and dishes of the Midlands tradition which flourished to the end of the seventeenth century and beyond. Ours was based rather on the sgraffito-decorated ware of North Devon, which is essentially a 'southern' style. Its nearest relations, in technical terms, are to be seen in early Byzantine and Islamic sgraffito wares, or those of Southern Europe and the Mediterranean Coasts.

My own ambition was not to revive any particular style but simply to make pots which could be used for all the ordinary purposes of daily living, and to be able to sell them at prices which would allow people to use them in their kitchens and not mind too much when they got broken. This implied that they must be made in appropriate quantities and fired in a big kiln; obviously a one-man, studio-scale operation would not be suitable. It was a fortunate chance that Elijah Comfort, the chief thrower formerly employed by Mr Beckett, was then still living in Winchcombe and was able to come back to work in the pottery. With him came a young boy, Sidney Tustin, who also after a few years became a good thrower. At firing times, this small group of three was increased by getting temporary helpers from Winchcombe, and in the later 1930s our strength was increased by the coming of Ray Finch and of Sidney's younger brother. We also had, even in those days, an occasional short-term student.

I thought at first that slipware was a simple kind of pottery, which would not be

Jar with three handles. Glazed stoneware,
greenish brown, Marks: MC and Abuja.
H 23cm *c.*1958. York City Art Gallery.

difficult to fire, but I soon found that galena, as a glaze material, has its own special difficulties. One of these was the sulphur it contains. Unless the ware is fired in the open, with the flames and gases passing freely over it, the glaze will not melt because the sulphur cannot escape; holes therefore had to be made in all the saggars to allow this to happen. These holes also admitted some of the fly-ash and sparks, contributing to the light and shade and life of the glazes; but they also sometimes caused rough or bare patches which made the pots quite unacceptable in most people's eyes.

A second difficulty with galena was that if the faggots were damp, or even the pots themselves not fully dry, the glaze refused to melt: the lead in the glaze seemed to volatilize, leaving dry areas or a rough surface, like coarse sandpaper, with an extremely unpleasant yellowish colour, like old, dry mustard.

Another drawback to slipware was porosity. For things like the big washing-pans made in the Becketts' time – which Elijah Comfort continued to make, up to about 1930 – this did not matter so much; but for pitchers and milk jugs, jars and flower-vases, porosity was a continuing cause of complaints from users, and we had to try various expedients in our attempts to overcome it. Earthenware has by definition a porous body as opposed to stoneware and porcelain, in which the body is vitrified or impermeable. The way to make earthenware watertight is by glazing it; but if there is crazing, water can pass through the network of fine cracks almost as easily as if there was no glaze at all; and our glazes were always crazed. The approved way to cure crazing is to give the pots a hard bisque fire before the glaze is applied; but this way out of the difficulty was not acceptable because I realised that it would spoil the beauty of the ware, the colours and quality of which depended on using a 'raw' (or 'slip', or *once-fired*) glaze, so that the operation of maturing the body and glaze could take place at the same time, not separately.

Later on I tried to eliminate porosity by firing at a higher temperature so as to make the body itself impermeable, even if the crazing was not cured. But I found that a limit is soon reached to what can be done in this direction. Earthenware

Two-handled 'Gwari' casserole. Glazed stoneware, dark brown speckled with green. Marks: MC and Abuja. D 37cm c.1960. Katharine Pleydell Bouverie.

clays usually will not vitrify properly; they start to fuse instead, become brittle, and may even slump or squat. As the old country potters used to say, 'The nature is fired out of the clay'. The pots also lose their fresh, bright colours and turn a dingy brown.

Faced with the limitations of this kind of ware, I began during the later nineteen-thirties to wish I had undertaken from the beginning to make stoneware rather than earthenware. Some of the features of Winchcombe slipware made during those years show evidence of this hankering for stoneware: the increasing use of black slip (partly in the hope that it would vitrify at our firing temperature), the designs scratched through the glaze and the underlying black slip to lay bare the raw clay of the pot, as in some T'zu-chou wares; or painted in black slip, again in imitation of T'zu-chou ware. By the early years of the second World War, I was feeling that most of the things I wanted to do in pottery could be done just as well, or better, in stoneware; many techniques of decoration are common to both, and some are much more satisfactory at the higher temperature.

In a time of peace it might have been a fairly simple matter to move over from slipware to stoneware. But during the first years of the second World War it was becoming extremely difficult to keep a small pottery going at all, and to embark on a radical change seemed to be impossible. In 1942, however, I was able to by-pass this problem. By an extraordinary sequence of good fortune I had the opportunity to make stoneware in a totally different context and environment, at Achimota College in Ghana (then known as the Gold Coast Colony). The idea of starting a pottery at Achimota was originally due to the inspiration of a remarkable man, Herbert Vladimir Meyerowitz, who was in charge of the Art School there. Two years before the war began, he had recruited Harry Davis from the Leach Pottery at St Ives; and by 1942, five years later, Harry Davis had evolved a successful stoneware clay-body from the rather unpromising local clays, and had perfected a range of stoneware glazes. For these, he used the natural raw materials of the country – pegmatites and other local igneous rocks, limestone, silica sand and of course wood ash from the ashpits of the small wood-fired kiln.

Stool with twelve pulled handles. Glazed stoneware, green and white. Marks: MC and Abuja (twice). H 34cm D 37cm c.1962. Katharine Pleydell Bouverie.

Four-handled jar with lid. Glazed
stoneware, red. Marked Abuja twice.
H 78cm *c.*1962. W. A. Ismay.

Thus, when I went out to Ghana to continue his work, there was never any question of making anything but stoneware.

It must not be supposed that the pottery which I took over at Achimota was anything like those pottery-studios which today are a normal adjunct to the Art Departments of Colleges in Europe and America. The pottery workers were not college students; the workshop was an efficient production unit, with three good throwers who had had two years of intensive training with Harry Davis and by this time were fully competent in all the processes involved, from the milling and preparation of the raw materials right through to the final firing. Six new apprentices had recently been taken on, who were already becoming good throwers, and there was a group of competent, semi-skilled supporting workers. In addition to the stoneware (as yet only being produced on a pilot scale) they were making thousands of unglazed terracotta water-coolers, which were much in demand and had by this time become a familiar and popular feature in the local markets. Building-bricks and roofing tiles were also being made on a small scale. Thus the Achimota Pottery Production Unit, far from being an exercise in academic self-expression, was a place where useful, needed things were being made, an exciting and entirely new development in local production for local needs, integrated with the life of the community as a whole.

Such indeed was its success that Meyerowitz had been able to persuade the Government, in Accra and London, to sponsor a much bigger enterprise. This included a brick-and-tile-works, already built and in operation at Alajo, three miles outside Achimota, which was now being enlarged in order to double its capacity. For the Pottery, an even more ambitious plan had been initiated; large buildings were already begun, and a number of machines were on order from Stoke-on-Trent, England – a very large ball mill, a blunger, pugmills, four power-driven throwing wheels, a jigger-and-jolley, and a lathe, all powered by a diesel engine. There were eight or nine other wheels, hand powered for the water-cooler makers. The plan included also the erection of four downdraught kilns, each of 28 cubic metres, though in the event only two of these were ever built.

Already in 1941 Meyerowitz, in a radio talk addressed to the people of Ghana, had said: 'The war has brought opportunities for development. . . . Shipping space had to be saved; imports had to be limited . . . so we built a tile factory and soon had a waiting-list of people wanting roofing tiles, glazed ware, drainpipes, water-coolers. . . . I believe all your traditional industries can be developed into new industries and used by the new generation. . . . As for the old artistic values, they will not be lost. They will come out in another form in the new work. . . . You are being called upon to be self-supporting. This may be your first step towards economic independence. . . . This is your golden opportunity. Do not let it slip past, it may take a lifetime to come again.'

Meyerowitz was a sculptor and wood carver, trained in Germany in the years 1919 to 1925. Like Gropius at the Bauhaus he saw the future of crafts to lie in re-establishing the essential unity of art and technology; and like Ananda Coomaraswamy, Eric Gill and more recently the author of *Zen and the Art of Motorcycle Maintenance,* he insisted that technology is simply the making of things; things properly made are beautiful by nature, and the time for re-unifying art and technology is long overdue. This being the philosophy underlying his scheme for developing local crafts into industries of the future, he sought out craftsmen whose thinking was somewhat along the same lines, like Harry Davis and myself, to help him translate the idea into actuality.

He did not try to import a properly trained industrial potter from Stoke-on-Trent, because in this brave and visionary project he was not aiming at anything so simplistic as straightforward industrialisation. The essence of his idea was that the new techniques and the increased scale of production must grow out of the old skills, and that an operation of this kind ought to be in the hands of a craftsman, that is to say an artist – this being the only species of person capable of restoring the unity of art and technology without distorting the human aspects of the operation. It is conceivable that the project might have succeeded if it had not been for the pressure of the war situation, which made it necessary to squeeze the delicate process of transition into too short a time-schedule – the expansion of the

Dish. Glazed stoneware, buff and blue.
Marks: stamped ABUJA and NIGERIA,
brush-drawn MC1965. W 45·5cm 1965.
W. A. Ismay.

Oil jar with screw top. Glazed stoneware,
greenish grey. Marks: MC and Wenford
Bridge. H 39cm *c.*1956. W. A. Ismay.

scale of operations was too sudden. Yet the paradox is that in the colonial context, the operation could never have been begun at all if it had not been for the pressures generated by the war.

When the war ended, the whole scheme was abandoned like any other emergency operation which was no longer needed for the war effort. Most of the craftsmen involved, West African and European, must think themselves lucky that they survived, and that the scars left behind were such as could be healed by the passing of a few years, or at the most a few decades; but Meyerowitz's death in June 1945 was a continuing and irreparable loss. Yet something of his original inspiration survived: in individuals, as a determination not to give up the struggle; in Governments, as a framework of *idées reçues*. Thus during the post-war years, 'Development' and 'Local Industries' quickly became accepted and respectable currency in the world of colonial adninistration. If it had not been so, the Government of Nigeria would not have been advertising for a potter in 1949, and I would not have had that second chance which occurs seldom in the lives of individuals anywhere, and almost never in Africa.

Colonies are (or were) essentially economic institutions. Nigeria in 1950, when I first went there, was still entirely *colonial* (more completely so, in fact, that the Ghana I had left in 1948) and the Europeans there (or most of them) would never have believed that it was to become an independent Republic only ten years later. I went there as a sort of Colonial Civil Servant, but one of a very low and humble grade; and anyone in that position who dared to recommend a development on grounds other than economic ones would not have lasted long. Like General Goering, most Colonial Administrators would have metaphorically felt for their revolvers if they heard the word 'Culture'; more quickly still, if anyone dared to pronounce the word 'Art'.

Not that I wanted to pronounce that fatal word. In the course of a four-thousand-word Survey on pottery prospects in Nigeria, which I wrote for the Department of Commerce and Industries soon after my arrival, I dismissed 'studio pottery and the so-called Art Ware' as irrelevancies; while of my admiration for the traditional pottery of the villages, I permitted myself only the observation that it was 'everywhere distinguished by simplicity and nobility in shape and decoration', and then hurried on to enlarge upon its practical merits which were underestimated at that time. My Survey went down well with the Department and with the Administration in general, especially in the Northern Provinces. Evidently my policy had succeeded. But I was not merely being cautious and politic. I agreed, and I still agree with the instincts of all my colleagues at that time, that it would have been irrelevant and in a sense, impertinent, to introduce concepts of art into my proposals.

What the 'art' element in pots really is, I do not know; nor I believe does anybody else, it being a great mystery: if you try to explore it verbally you will be sure to misrepresent it. It is infinitely more important to learn how to make the things. Whether pots are good or bad in a technical and practical way is a thing in which it is possible to acquire some knowledge and some degree of control; but as to whether they are good or bad in their real character and their inner life – this is something which is not in the control of any intellectual system but can only be perceived directly.

The character of the stoneware made at Vumé and at Abuja was always strongly determined by the local clays, and since these always had a rather high content of iron oxide, it was necessary to make a virtue of necessity and to explore the wide range of colour and tone which can be obtained with such materials. During most of my time there we had no plastic white-firing clay for making a white slip, and so for sgraffito decoration we used a black slip (lateritic ironstone mixed with the local clay) which was even darker than the body itself. We also used a clear, transparent glaze which on a white body would have given a pale celadon colour, but on ours produced a much deeper colour, almost a bottle-green, like deep clear water, with glowing touches of iron red at the edges where the glaze is thinner and the iron oxide from the underlying clay takes possession. Under this glaze we sometimes used a non-plastic white slip, a fifty-fifty mixture of kaolin and feldspar, which enabled us to inlay the incised decoration so that there was a contrast

Casserole. Glazed stoneware, brown and buff. Marks: MC and Wenford Bridge. D 26·5cm c.1971. W. A. Ismay.

between the dark green of the body and the pale celadon of the inlaid design.

Lighter colours became possible when we obtained zircon sand from the tin-mines of the Jos Plateau, and found that our ball mill could grind it fine enough for an opaque glaze, thus providing a white ground for painted decoration in brown (iron) and blue (cobalt). Cobalt carbonate was the only material which we ever had to import from abroad, and of this we only used a few ounces each year.

An entirely new extension of our range of stoneware colours was the vivid opalescent blue, which is not due to cobalt or to any other colouring oxide but is a purely 'optical' effect of the interference of light-waves; hence it requires a dark ferruginous background material to develop its full intensity. This discovery was the result of a combination of happy accident with patient study of an entirely 'unconventional' material, the whiteish, coral-like masses which used to accumulate in the ashpits of the wood-fired kiln. It is evidently a fused wood-ash, a glassy slag or scoria which forms where the temperature of the ashpits is high enough, if the ash itself has a high content of silica (a characteristic of the local hardwood ashes). Under these conditions it will fuse, and turn into slag or clinker. We ground this new material in the ball mill and used thirty to thirty-five per cent of it in a glaze-batch which gave this vivid 'optical blue', provided the firing conditions were suitable. This colour has now become the main characteristic of Abuja stoneware and is easily the most popular with the Nigerian public.

Most of the Abuja stoneware was biscuit-fired before glazing, but I also developed an interesting 'slip-glaze' containing grass-ash as well as the wood-ash slag. This fired a clear, transparent, warm brown on the local clay, an effect which was somewhat similar to the golden browns of the slipware we used to make at Winchcombe during the 1920s and 30s. I used it on the plain dark body, scratching the decoration through the glaze to the raw clay but owing to the lack of a reliable white slip I was unable to develop its full potential for sgraffito decoration.

A glaze of the same type, containing grass-ash, local wood-ash slag and a high

Two-handled 'Gwari' casserole. Glazed stoneware, brown. Marks: MC and Wenford Bridge. D 32cm *c*.1973. W. A. Ismay.

proportion of clay, is the main one used here since my return to Cornwall in 1965. Over a white slip the golden brown is lighter in tone, and where the dark body is exposed it tends towards a black *tenmoku*. Thus the 'post-West-Africa' stoneware made at Wenford Bridge represents, after many years of searching, a kind of return to the beginnings, and to the idea, conceived during the 1930s that slipware techniques, and even the warmth of slipware colours, could be translated into the new dimension of stoneware.

Michael Cardew: Chronology

1901	May, born in Wimbledon.
	Family holiday house at Saunton, North Devon.
	Family visits to Fremington pottery of Edwin Beer Fishley (d. 1911).
	London and Devon homes contain functional and decorative Fremington wares.
1919–23	At Exeter College, Oxford.
1921–22	Learns to throw at Braunton Pottery managed by William Fishley Holland, grandson of E. B. Fishley.
1922	First learns of Bernard Leach's St Ives Pottery from article in *The Pottery Gazette* accidentally seen at Braunton.
1923	January, visits St Ives; meets Shoji Hamada and Bernard Leach; asks to join pottery.
	July, joins St Ives as Leach's first English pupil.
	September–October, travels to Venice, Cairo, Istanbul, Athens.
1924	Katharine Pleydell Bouverie pupil at St Ives.
1925	Norah Braden pupil at St Ives.
1926	June, leaves St Ives, rents abandoned pottery at Greet, near Winchcombe in Gloucestershire.
	Employs Elijah Comfort, previously chief thrower at pottery and Sidney Tustin as boy apprentice. Develops range of slip glazed earthenware.
1928–30	Exhibits at Philip Mairet's New Handworker Gallery, Percy Street, London.
	Work bought by Sydney Greenslade (eventually bequeathed to University College of Wales, Aberystwyth).
1931	Joins National Society of Painters, Sculptors, Engravers and Potters.
	Exhibitions at Royal Institute Galleries, Piccadilly.
1933	Marries Mariel Russell.
	Charlie Tustin joins pottery as apprentice.
	Exhibits at Muriel Rose's Little Gallery, Ennis Street, and at Heals, London.
1934	November, Seth Cardew born.
1936	Ray Finch joins pottery as apprentice.
	Cornelius Cardew born.

1938	Works privately for six weeks at Copeland factory, Stoke-on-Trent, making tea-sets in 'fine earthenware'.
	Ennis Cardew born.
	Exhibition at Brygos Gallery, Bond Street, London, includes the three 'fountain' bowls.
1939	Leaves Winchcombe in hands of partner Ray Finch.
	Buys Wenford Bridge, on the edge of Bodmin Moor, Cornwall.
	Builds smaller version of Winchcombe kiln. Plans to maintain Wenford Bridge and Winchcombe as sister potteries.
1941–2	Brief return to Winchcombe Pottery.
1942	To Achimota College, Gold Coast Colony (now Ghana) as pottery instructor in H. V. Meyerowitz's scheme to develop local skills into self-supporting industries: quantity production of bricks, tiles, and stoneware pots using local materials at Alajo.
1945	Achimota scheme stops.
	With three African students goes to Vumé-Dugamé on the Lower Volta River in the Gold Coast Colony. Builds the Volta Pottery, makes stoneware.
	Sells Winchcombe Pottery business to Ray Finch.
1947	Vumé pots exhibited by British Council in Accra.
1948	Forced by illness to return to England.
	Exhibition of work from Volta Pottery at brother Philip's house, 20 Regent's Park Terrace, London.
1949	Adds downdraught first chamber to Wenford Bridge kiln to make stoneware.
	Ivan McMeekin joins pottery as partner.
	Accepts post as Pottery Officer in Department of Industry and Commerce, Nigeria.
1950	Travels throughout Northern Nigeria.
	Spends ten months of the year in Nigeria, remaining time at Wenford Bridge.
	November, exhibition of his stoneware pottery made at Wenford Bridge, at Berkeley Galleries, Davies Street, London.

1951	Recommends building Pottery Training Centre at Abuja. Site chosen in August. Promoted Senior Pottery Officer.
1952	April, Abuja Centre opens with six African trainees.
1958	February–March, exhibition of stoneware pottery made by him at Abuja, at Berkeley Galleries.
1959	September–October, exhibition of stoneware pottery by him and pupils at Abuja, at Berkeley Galleries.
1960	Exhibition of Abuja Pottery in Lagos.
1962	June–July, exhibition of stoneware pottery by him and pupils at Abuja, at Berkeley Galleries.
	Exhibition of stoneware by him and pupils at Abuja, at Galerie La Borne, rue Durantin, Paris.
1965	Retires from Nigeria.
	Awarded MBE
	Returns to Wenford Bridge.
1967	First visit to USA, University of Wisconsin.
1968	January–March, lectures and demonstrations in New Zealand.
	April–May, lectures in Australia.
	May–November, to Darwin in Northern Territory of Australia to help Ivan McMeekin set up pottery training centre for Aborigines.
	December, brief visit to Abuja.
1969	*Pioneer Pottery* published by Longman Group Ltd.
1971	Eldest son Seth joins Wenford Bridge Pottery.
	Pioneer Pottery published in USA by St Martin's Press.
	Alister Hallum makes film *Abuja Pottery*.
1973	Visits Vumé-Dugamé and Abuja during making of Arts Council film *Mud and Water Man* directed by Alister Hallum.
1975	Exhibition at Craftsman Potter's Association, Marshall Street, London.
1976	May, retrospective touring exhibition organised by the Crafts Advisory Committee, opens at Boymans van-Beuningen Museum, Rotterdam.

Pottery marks

St. Ives 1923–26

Winchcombe 1926–39

Wenford Bridge 1939-41, 1949 onwards

Volta 1945–48

Abuja 1952–65

Bibliography

ANONYMOUS ('a Cornish correspondent') 'Notice of Bernard Leach's first exhibition in London' in *Pottery Gazette and Glass Trade Review*, 1 March 1923.

BREARS Peter C. D. *The English Country Pottery: its history and techniques*, Newton Abbot, David and Charles, 1971.

CARDEW Michael A. 'Bernard Leach' in *The Studio*, November 1925.

CARDEW Michael A. Preface to *A Potter's Book* by Bernard Leach, London, 1940 (14th imp. 1973).

CARDEW Michael A. 'Industry and the Studio Potter' in *Crafts* II, 1, London, The Red Rose Guild of Craftsmen, 1942.

CARDEW Michael A. *Stoneware Pottery*, pamphlet associated with the exhibition of his work, London Berkeley Galleries, November 1950.

CARDEW Michael A. 'Nigerian Traditional Pottery' in *Nigeria Quarterly* 39, 1952.

CARDEW Michael A. 'Pioneer Pottery at Abuja' in *Nigeria Quarterly* 52, 1956.

CARDEW Michael A. 'Potting in Northern Nigeria' in *Pottery Quarterly* III, 1956.

CARDEW Michael A. *Stoneware Pottery*, pamphlet associated with exhibition of his work made at Abuja, London, Berkeley Galleries, February–March 1958.

CARDEW Michael A. *Stoneware Pottery*, pamphlet associated with exhibition of work by Cardew and his pupils at Abuja, London, Berkeley Galleries, September–October 1959.

CARDEW Michael A. 'Bernard Leach: recollections' in *Essays in appreciation of Bernard Leach* (special issue of *New Zealand Potter*), 1960.

CARDEW Michael A. 'Firing the big pot at Kwali' in *Nigeria Quarterly* 70, September 1961.

CARDEW Michael A. *Stoneware Pottery* pamphlet associated with exhibition of work by Cardew and his pupils at Abuja, London, Berkeley Galleries, June–July 1962.

CARDEW Michael A. 'Traditional Pottery. The Pottery Training Centre', in *A Chronicle of Abuja*, pp.41–50, Lagos, African Universities Press, 2nd ed. 1962.

CARDEW Michael A. 'Design' in *Currency* (the magazine of the Australian Reserve Bank), July 1969.

CARDEW Michael A. *Pioneer Pottery*. London, Longman, 1969, 1975 and New York, St Martin's Press, 1971.

CARDEW Michael A. Introduction in Sylvia Leith Ross, *Nigerian Pottery*, Ibadan, 1970.

CARDEW Michael A. *Life as a Potter* pamphlet (11 pp.) published by America Crafts Council as result of their Southeast workshop at Arrowmount School, Gatlinburg, Tennessee, June 1971.

CARDEW Michael A. 'Potters and amateur potters' in *Pottery Quarterly* x, 38, 1971. (Similar to 4pp pamphlet published under same title by the USA National Council on Education for the Ceramic Arts.)

CARDEW Michael A. 'Ladi Kwali' in *Craft Horizons,* New York, American Crafts Council, April 1972.

CARDEW Michael A. 'A view of African pottery' in *Ceramic Monthly*, Feb. 1974.

CARDEW Michael A. 'What pots mean to me' in *Ceramic Review* 32, Mar.–Apr. 1975.

CASSON Michael *Pottery in Britain Today*, London 1967.

COUNTS Charles 'Michael Cardew' in *Craft Horizons,* February 1972.

DIGBY G. R. Wingfield 'British contemporary pottery' in *House and Garden*, VI, X, pp 32, 90, 1951.

DIGBY G. R. Wingfield *The Work of the Modern Potter in England*, London, 1952.

FAGG William and PICTON John *The Potter's Art in Africa*, London, The British Museum, 1970.

HENNELL Thomas *The Countryman at Work*, London, Architectural Press, 1947 (Collection of articles from the *Architectural Review*. 'The potter' described work at Winchcombe Pottery).

HOLLAND William FISHLEY *Fifty years a potter*, London, *Pottery Quarterly* special publication, 1958.

JEWITT Llewellyn *Ceramic art of Great Britain,* London 1878.

LEACH Bernard *A Potter's Book*, London, Faber, 1940 (14th imp. 1973).

LEACH Bernard *The Leach pottery (at St Ives) 1920–46* pamphlet associated with exhibition at the Berkeley Galleries, London 1946.

LEACH Bernard *A Potter's portfolio*, London, Lund Humphries, 1951. Reissued with alterations as *The Potter's challenge*, New York, E. P. Dutton, 1975 and London, Souvenir Press, 1976.

LEITH ROSS Sylvia *Nigerian Pottery*. A catalogue of specimens shown in the Jos Museum. Ibadan University Press, 1970.

LOMAX Charles J. *Quaint Old English Pottery* London, 1909.

MARRIOTT Charles *British Handicrafts*. Vol. XIII of *British Life and Thought*, London, British Council, 1943.

MARSH Ernest 'Michael Cardew: a potter of Winchcombe, Gloucestershire' in *Apollo*, March 1943.

MEYEROWITZ Herbert Vladimir *A report on the possibilities of the development of village crafts in Basutoland*, Morija 1936.

O'BRIEN Michael 'Abuja after Michael Cardew' in *Ceramic Review* 34, July–August 1975.

PLEYDELL BOUVERIE Katharine 'At St Ives in the Early Years' in *Essays in appreciation of Bernard Leach* (special issue of *New Zealand Potter*), 1960.

PLEYDELL BOUVERIE Katharine 'Michael Cardew: a personal account' in *Ceramic Review* 20, March–April 1973. (Reprinted in this volume.)

ROSE Muriel *The Artist Potter in England*, London, Faber, 1955 (2nd ed. 1970).

STICHBURY Peter 'The Abuja scene' in *New Zealand Potter* II, 2, December 1959.

STRONG, H. W. *Industries of North Devon*. Introduced by B. D. Hughes, Newton Abbot, David & Charles, 1971. (A reprint of the 1889 publication.)

Films

Abuja Pottery – Alister Hallum director, 1971.

Mud and Water Man – Alister Hallum director, 1973. Produced by the Arts Council of Great Britain. (Filmed with Cardew at the Wenford Bridge, Volta and Abuja Potteries.)

Index

*Page numbers in italics refer
to captions*